What Student Should Know About Reading a Novel

Paula Bryant Bonilla

PEARSON

Boston   Columbus   Indianapolis   New York   San Francisco   Upper Saddle River
Amsterdam   Cape Town   Dubai   London   Madrid   Milan   Munich   Paris   Montreal   Toronto
Delhi   Mexico City   São Paulo   Sydney   Hong Kong   Seoul   Singapore   Taipei   Tokyo

Senior Sponsoring Editor: Katharine Glynn
Director of Marketing: Megan Galvin-Fak
Senior Supplements Editor: Donna Campion
Project Coordination, Text Design, and Electronic Page Makeup: Grapevine Publishing Services, Inc.
Cover Designer: Alison Barth Burgoyne
Senior Manufacturing Buyer: Roy Pickering
Printer and Binder: Courier Westford
Cover Printer: Moore Langen Division of Courier

Copyright © 2013 Pearson Education, Inc.

All rights reserved. Printed in the United States of America. This publication is protected by Copyright and permission should be obtained from the publisher prior to any prohibited reproduction, storage in a retrieval system, or transmission in any form or by any means, electronic, mechanical, photocopying, recording, or likewise. To obtain permission(s) to use material from this work, please submit a written request to Pearson Education, Inc., Permissions Department, One Lake Street, Upper Saddle River, New Jersey 07458 or you may fax your request to 201-236-3290.

Please visit us at www.pearsonhighered.com

1 2 3 4 5 6 7 8 9 10—V013—13 12

ISBN 13: 978-0-205-87052-3
ISBN 10:   0-205-87052-X

PEARSON   www.pearsonhighered.com

Contents

To the Student v

Chapter 1: *What Novels Do 1*
Narrative: What makes a story? 2
Using the novel: Interpretation of life 4
Using the novel: Entertainment or escape 7
Using the novel: Propaganda or political commentary 8
Using the novel: Expressing the times 10
Putting this chapter to work 11

Chapter 2: *How Novels Work 13*
Premise 13
Setting 15
Plot 16
Characters and dialogue 18
Narrative mode or point of view 19
Theme 22
Symbolism 23
Putting this chapter to work 25

Chapter 3: *Recognize Types of Novels 26*
Romantic novels 27
Realistic novels 27
Naturalistic novels 28
Avant-garde novels 29
Gothic novels 30
Coming-of-age novels 30
Detective novels 31
Western novels 32
Dystopian novels 33
Other types of novels 34
Putting this chapter to work 36

Chapter 4: *Respond Actively to Novels*   37
Previewing a novel   38
Marking up a novel   39
Student annotated reading sample from Kate Chopin's *The Awakening*   41
E-books   42
Journaling about a novel   42
Talking about a novel   43
Take a second look at the novel   46
Putting this chapter to work   47

Chapter 5: *Discover Ideas for Writing about Novels*   48
Thesaurus search   49
Similes   49
Freewriting   50
Pro and con lists   50
Cubing   50
Rock or feather?   51
Probing questions   52
Cluster and flow   53
Putting this chapter to work   56

TO THE STUDENT

College offers students ways of seeing the world and its countless possibilities. A novel works in the same way. It's natural, then, that reading good novels is part of the territory of higher education, no matter what your ultimate major or career goal.

Whether it is classic or contemporary, a gothic horror or a western adventure, a chilling view of the future or a hopeful look at the present, a novel is a world complete with its own culture, landmarks, and viewpoints. When you head for a new vacation destination, you probably take along an insider's guidebook. After all, with tips and advice at the ready, you can start exploring that much faster and get more out of your trip. In the same way as a map or insider's guide, this book, *What Every Student Should Know About Reading a Novel*, will fortify you with the tools you need to enter the world of a novel prepared for the journey, savvy about what to look for, and ready to communicate about what you've experienced.

How to use this book

Use this book as you would any guidebook: Flip through it, reread it, write in it, wear it out, and definitely bring it with you on your travels through unfamiliar literary territory. Get to know its content before you start your novel-reading assignment, and then keep it handy throughout your novel reading. Lost? Curious? Check this book again. And again.

What Every Student Should Know About Reading a Novel will give you a framework for understanding how to approach, enjoy, and interpret any novel your instructor might assign or that you might encounter in college courses. In Chapter One, you'll discover what novels of all kinds are designed to do for you, the reader. Chapter Two exposes the novel's inner workings and how their structure empowers novels to make meaning.

In Chapter Three, you'll identify the common types of novels, such as coming of age, epistolary, and dystopian, deciding what you like about them and getting clued in on what to expect as you read. Chapter Four offers a fresh take on the idea of reading actively, giving advice and examples you can use about how to respond to novels at the college level.

Finally, in Chapter Five, you'll get a taste of what it means to be a powerful communicator about the fictional worlds you've explored. Use this chapter as a springboard for college writing assignments to come, sampling the selection of classic and innovative idea-generating activities it offers.

Features

What Every Student Should Know About Reading a Novel offers a pair of inviting, efficient features that work together:

1. *Accessible content.* This book is easy to follow and fun to read. It presents technical terms in an engaging, easy-to-understand way, using examples you can relate to your own life. At the same time, it doesn't talk down to you, but presents everything you need to get started on reading a novel at the college level, without discouraging you with a flood of detail or frustrating you with overly simplistic explanations.

2. *Bulleted checklists.* You'll see these tools throughout the book. Each chapter begins with a bulleted list of what you'll expect to gain. And each chapter ends with a series of provocative questions. You can apply these questions to any novel you're reading. Plus, important points are broken down into bulleted lists as they come up, signposting your learning as you go.

Acknowledgments

I would like to thank my senior sponsoring editor, Katharine Glynn, for her outstanding support, feedback, and guidance. I would also like to thank assistant editor Rebecca Gilpin for her unfailing communication skills and good cheer, and Dianne Hall for her unflappable expertise in managing the design and production. And a special thanks goes to my family of novel readers.

1

WHAT NOVELS DO

In this chapter, you will:

- Recognize that the storytelling impulse is universal
- Trace the origins of the impulse to tell stories
- Learn how narrative makes a story
- Discover the uses of the novel and how to identify them
- Understand how reading novels can benefit you

Look at yourself in a reflective surface—a pool of water, a car's side view mirror, the bowl of a metal spoon. Do you see yourself clearly, or is the image blurred, or even upside down? William Shakespeare once wrote that an actor holds a mirror up to nature. A good novel holds a mirror up to life, reflecting an image—slanted or straight—of what it's like to be alive.

In college, you will be asked to read novels and communicate what you think of the images of life they reflect. Opening a novel can be like looking into a mirror. This guide will give you an idea of what to expect from the image it reflects and how to interpret it at the college level.

When you pick up a novel for the first time, you're probably not inclined to study its working parts, such as plot and theme. Instead, you are more likely to question what the novel does—its purpose. This first chapter will take a look at the lasting impact of the novel.

Narrative: What makes a story?

A novel is defined as an invented narrative of considerable length that deals imaginatively with human experience, usually through a connected sequence of events involving a group of persons in a specific setting. But in simplest terms, a novel is a story.

We all tell stories. Here's one: A college student (call her Jen) working part-time at a retail store in a major city experiences a certain mysterious event on the way home from work one dark winter evening. On the train, she suddenly sees a cell phone slip from the pocket of a shaggy-haired boy with a worried look and a handkerchief tied around his right hand. She notices an expensively dressed older woman seated behind the boy lean forward, grab the cell phone, and shove it into her own coat pocket. No one else appears to witness the theft.

Jen starts to speak up, but keeps quiet without knowing exactly why. The boy gets off at the next stop, apparently without realizing his phone is missing. The thief, wobbling in high-heeled boots, gets off at the same stop and appears to follow him.

When Jen comes home to her apartment and greets her roommate, a college sophomore (call her Marley), she will no doubt tell Marley the story of what happened on her way home. Jen will describe the scene for Marley (the shuddering motion of the train, the flickering overhead lights, the rows of empty seats). She will describe the characters (the preoccupied and possibly injured boy, the sinister smirk of the older woman with her orangey lipstick, herself as a silent witness).

And she will guess at those characters' motivations for doing what they did: Were the innocent-looking boy and the wealthy-looking woman terrorists handing off a cell-phone bomb ready to detonate? Or was the boy a runaway from a foster home? Was the woman a kleptomaniac who couldn't stop herself from stealing? Why did the woman follow the boy? What might have happened to the boy to make him so spacey that he didn't realize he had been robbed? And why didn't Jen herself manage to speak up at the time?

Jen's narration of this incident will probably capture Marley's total attention. She will stop chopping the onion for dinner and sit down on the couch, ready to hear more.

Jen will oblige her audience of one with more detail, more speculation, more commentary: "The boy's eyes looked red, as if he had been crying, or had maybe just been sprayed with pepper spray. What if the woman already knew him and wanted to erase text messages on his phone that she herself had left there confessing to some sort of crime? And it's possible I didn't say anything because the woman reminded me of my mother, who died last spring, and I felt a weird connection with her somehow."

Jen and Marley, storyteller and audience, are entertained by this narrative, but the incident has also started them both wondering. Such is the power of narrative that *you* might be wondering at the moment you read this, What would I have done? Would I have gotten involved? What does this situation remind me of in my own life? Can a story contribute anything to the way I live my life now, or the way I want to live it? If it can, how can it do that?

Jen's story of the strangers on the train is a narrative about something that really happened. A novel is a fictional—made-up—narrative that sparks our imagination about something having to do with our shared human experience. The urge to tell stories is ancient. Why? Because the basic urge to talk about and understand ourselves as human beings is as old as humanity itself.

Stories are meant to be shared. Jen could have kept her story to herself, and then gone to her room, curled up under a blanket, and scribbled it into a private journal. But instead, she played a role similar to a novelist, using words to craft a scene for Marley to ponder.

That urge to tell stories makes Jen not very different from a primitive storyteller of ancient times. These storytellers told tales of adventure and brave accomplishments to a group gathered around a communal fire. The stories gave voice to people's doubts, fears, pleasures, and plans as they geared up for a battle or a festival, mourned a dead hero, or celebrated a hard-won victory.

When that long-ago audience let those tales come alive in their minds and hearts, they participated in a give-and-take interaction with the storyteller. They let the story tell them something about themselves. The storyteller's job, then and today, is to express people's deepest desires, to show people what their wants and needs reveal about who they are, and perhaps to spur people to keep going forward as best they can in the life struggle all people have in common.

The novel as we know it today has its roots in an ancient genre, or type of artistic work, called the epic. (*Epic* is a word we still use today to mean "larger than life," or "impressive.") The epic was a long narrative poem spinning the imaginary adventures of a hero who was courageous, strong, and intelligent, but not necessarily always good.

One of the most famous early epics is *Gilgamesh*. It tells of a superhero-like king, a bad boy who was so powerful and destructive that the gods were afraid of him. They decided to create an alter ego (the kinder, gentler Enkidu) to fight with him. The spectacular wrestling match of Gilgamesh and Enkidu ends in a tie.

It was an adrenaline-fueled storyline, but it also could have made listeners think: perhaps people need personalities that include both aggression and compassion in order to survive this wild and dangerous world.

Any novel in a bookstore or on your e-reader today is not so far removed from that dramatic story of 2700 B.C.E. That's because, in addition to provoking questions about timeless issues, *Gilgamesh* thrilled and unsettled its audiences by owning all of the benefits of the best fiction (or literary work of the imagination): adventure, struggle, conquest and defeat, thorny human relationships.

Good novels—like those you will be reading before, during, and even after college—are tricky packages. When you open them, they explode with all the same ancient elements of excitement, mystery, and satisfaction of the epic of the warring superheroes of *Gilgamesh*.

Using the novel: Interpretation of life

Novels have a purpose: They are written to be used. One use, or reason for being, of the novel is the interpretation of life. Novels aren't written to teach you lessons, like those gruesome cautionary tales in which children who break rules or tell lies tumble to their deaths or are devoured by wild beasts. But novels definitely communicate a certain take on life, even while they aim to please readers with a gripping, enjoyable story.

A novelist can put a positive spin on his or her interpretation of life. That is, the novel can have a happy ending, like those romantic comedy movies that end with weddings. Of course, happy endings aren't always true to life. As Oscar Wilde commented in one of his plays, *The Importance of Being Earnest* (1895), in unrealistically optimistic novels, the good characters end up happily and the bad characters end up unhappily, and "that is why it is called fiction."

One example of a novelist who interprets, or presents a picture, of life as basically fair and decent is Jane Austen. Her novels about proper English families, written in the nineteenth century, are still popular with readers today. Austen's novels present life as orderly and comfortable; it is only when characters break the rules for correct behavior that things go wrong.

Did Austen really see the world as a perfect country garden? Probably not. Instead, the carefully arranged picture of social life she presents to us, her readers, is simply an image of the way she and others of her time *wished* life could be. Austen knew life was complicated. Her novels, such as *Pride and Prejudice* (1813) and *Emma* (1815), are her way of presenting an ideal possible world that is easy to understand and to control, in which self-centered and insensitive people get punished, and good people, even though they might face a shortage of money here or a challenge in finding a mate there, are always rewarded before the last page.

Other interpretations of life you will read about in novels can be bitter. Many nineteenth-century novels were gloomy and pessimistic. They showed, through the development of narrative events, that life was not fair at all and that evil people were likely to triumph.

A twentieth-century example of this dark worldview is John Steinbeck's 1937 novel *Of Mice and Men*. It paints a picture of human life that is lonely and predatory, with the strong preying on the weak. Does Steinbeck intend to present a depressing interpretation of life? Maybe not. Steinbeck's worldview seems to be a little more complicated than "the oppressor always wins." His characters appear to be at the mercy of their limited circumstances. And yet, in spite of life's hostility, Lennie and George manage to maintain a positive friendship, even though it ends tragically. Perhaps Steinbeck is suggesting: No matter what the odds are against having a relationship that isn't based on using or being used, brotherly love is still possible.

For another example of a pessimistic interpretation of life, think about the TV drama series *Breaking Bad*. The chemistry teacher turned methamphetamine manufacturer, Walter White, might have stepped straight out of a Thomas Hardy novel, given the painfully obsessive way he keeps making all the wrong choices (drug trafficking, murder) for all the right reasons (love for his wife, a desire to support his family financially). We care about White, in spite of our better judgment, but we also understand why his choices bring him so much grief. Perhaps Steinbeck would have agreed that if White didn't have a good conscience to begin with, he wouldn't find himself in such a jam.

Another popular interpretation of life, presented by many novels since World War II, is the idea that life is absurd and people are at the mercy of random events. This is a 180-degree turn from the optimistic belief in an orderly, predictable world celebrated by Austen.

It also contradicts the viewpoint of twentieth-century novelists such as Graham Greene (*The End of the Affair* [1951], *The Quiet American* [1955]), who present the world as filled with evil and injustice but as still positive, governed by a loving God whose ultimate plan we can never fully know.

One classic and darkly hilarious novel of the absurd is Joseph Heller's war novel *Catch-22* (1961). An American World War II bombardier named Yossarian and his fellow pilots are condemned to fly a never-ending round of dangerous combat missions due to a military rule known as Catch-22. The rule states that anyone who is crazy can ask to be grounded, but any pilot who worries about being safe must be sane, and thus, not being crazy at all, must continue to fly more missions.

Yossarian finally finds out that there is no such rule as Catch-22. But because everyone believes the rule exists, it must be followed. In fact, because it doesn't exist, the rule can never be overthrown. The narrative presents Heller's interpretation of life—that perhaps the only way to survive an insane system is to become insane oneself.

But did Heller himself really believe that? If he did, *Catch-22* would probably not have been written, and its developing story of pilots fumbling to make choices of right and wrong would not resonate so well with millions of readers. Perhaps one of the hopeful questions the novel raises is: If we know something is crazy, could that be the first step toward sanity?

Using the novel: Entertainment or escape

Many novelists write in the hope that their readers (and they themselves) might learn something about what is to be human, even if nobody discovers the fabled meaning of life. But what about when a reader just wants to kick back with a great story?

Entertainment and escape from the ball-and-chain sameness of everyday reality are perfectly good reasons to read novels. And novelists are certainly motivated to write them for that reason.

In the eighteenth and nineteenth centuries, novels had a bad reputation. They were often so much fun to read that an educated person was embarrassed to be caught reading one. In fact, many eighteenth-century novelists disguised their fiction as true stories or memoirs: for example, Jonathan Swift's *Gulliver's Travels* and Daniel Defoe's *Robinson Crusoe*. Reading fiction was considered a vulgar waste of time. Then why did so many people read novels? Because it felt good to escape reality.

At the turn of the twentieth century, favorite entertainments for the ordinary U.S. citizen including attending circuses and Wild West tent shows, and going to stage melodramas about evil landlords and dainty damsels in distress (audiences were advised to bring along plenty of hankies to cry into). And instead of great plays and poetry, most people read serialized fiction in popular magazines.

These magazines ran sensationalized stories in several parts, each with a cliffhanger ending that left the main character in danger. This was a simple strategy to motivate readers to keep subscribing to—or buying the next issue of—the magazine in order to pick up the thread of the story.

These illustrated periodicals were printed on cheap paper and were aimed at working-class young people. In England, they were known as penny dreadfuls because they could be bought for a penny and their subject matter was usually horror or crime fiction. Later, penny dreadfuls expanded their focus to include unrealistic rags-to-riches stories of poor boys who struck it rich through their own cleverness.

In the United States, these serialized publications were known as dime novels, and they usually told of the rip-roaring deeds of cowboys such as Buffalo Bill and Deadeye Dick. The penny dreadful and dime novel evolved into the comic book of today.

The twentieth century definitely has its own escapist fiction, from Ian Fleming's James Bond spy novels, to the Harold Robbins and Jacqueline Susann novels recounting the over-the-top sexual exploits of the rich and ruthless, to horror thrillers such as *The Silence of the Lambs* by Thomas Harris, to the so-called chick lit novels such as *Confessions of a Shopaholic* or *The Devil Wears Prada*, to the recent anti-heroine detective novel *The Girl with the Dragon Tattoo* and its sequels.

Living out our fantasies of facing death fearlessly, becoming rich and famous, or single-handedly saving civilization without mussing our hair or creasing our tuxedo is a legitimate occupation for our spare time—after all, we recognize the daydream for what it is.

Given that it is no crime to entertain ourselves, though, we might as well choose the best of the genre. Good escapist novels, although they don't pretend to interpret reality for us in any life-changing way, are well crafted and present us with characters who are believable and true to life.

Such novels capture our attention by charming us and involving us as we sink into the dream of the narrative with delight, like biting into the sweetest and richest of cheesecakes. It's a guilty pleasure, but why not indulge once in a while? Some of the best escapist fiction might even communicate a truth or two about life while entertaining the reader. Try a John le Carré spy novel or Anne Rice's 1976 novel *Interview with the Vampire* for some good high-calorie escapes that nevertheless have some nutritional value.

Using the novel:
Propaganda or political commentary

Another use of the novel is as propaganda. The term *propaganda* often has a negative association, but its meaning is neutral: the spreading of ideas, information, or rumor for the purpose of helping or injuring an institution, a cause, or a person. Novelists are usually sharp observers of society and of human nature. It is only natural that certain novelists throughout history have tried to use their art to help spark social change, for better or worse.

The antislavery classic, *Uncle Tom's Cabin* (1852), by the American author Harriet Beecher Stowe, is one of the most impressive novels written—not because of the artistry of its writing style, which is melodramatic and sentimental, but because of the amazing role it played in the outbreak of the Civil War. As soon as Stowe's novel rolled off the printing presses, defenders of slavery shouted in protest and abolitionists burst out in praise. The book was read the world over.

Many literary scholars of the nineteenth century wanted to see, in *Uncle Tom's Cabin*'s success, evidence that novels have the power to bring about social change. It may or may not be possible for a novel to change the world; what can be said for certain is that Stowe's narrative exposing the immorality of slavery was the number one best-selling novel of the entire nineteenth century, and it is still read and written about today.

Stowe's novel is more than propaganda. That is, it doesn't stop at merely taking a stand against the institution of slavery or stirring up public feeling against it. The story also deals with our own basic human tendency to oppress each other. That's a timeless issue that makes Stowe's novel more than just a political statement.

Other novels work in the same way—taking a stand on a social problem but also commenting on the flaws in our own human nature that brought it about. Charles Dickens's *Oliver Twist* (1838) criticized the inhumane practice of forcing people who cannot pay their debts to live in poorhouses. And Laura Z. Hobson's *Gentleman's Agreement* (1947) exposed the concealed anti-Semitism in American middle-class social circles in the 1940s.

One example of the downside of using a novel for political commentary is when a writer uses his or her work of fiction as a weapon to attack a group, rather than to dramatize an issue. In 1832, an angry anti-Catholic mob burned down a convent near Boston. Three years later, when the rioters were being tried for the crime, Rebecca Reed published a horror novel titled *Six Months in a Convent*. As the fictional setting for her main character's imprisonment and mistreatment, Reed chose the very convent that had been attacked by the mob. The novel sold 200,000 copies in one month thanks to the timely connection of its publication with the trial's newspaper coverage, and it fanned the fire of anti-Catholic sentiment in the United States.

When you read a present-day novel that uses fiction to attack a social institution such as a religion or an ethnic group, it can be hard not to be pulled into the drama—and internalize the message. When you read exaggerated, harsh, or unlikely accounts of a segment of society in a fictional context, why not think of it as a red flag? It can signal you to check out other sources before making up your own mind about the issue. Also, consider the source: Do you think that this particular author might have a personal agenda, an axe to grind?

Using the novel: Expressing the times

Think back on your life: Is there any common thread that you can see running through it? Do you miss the customs and fashions of any particular decade of your life—say, the nineties? Was there any particular social group you belonged to (cheerleading, band camp) that you will never forget? Do you identify with a particular religious, political, or ethnic group (Muslim, Democrat, Latina) with its own distinct qualities?

The intellectual, moral, and cultural climate of a particular time period—the spirit of an era—is known as its zeitgeist, from the German words for "time" and "spirit." When you read a novel set in a certain time period, its author can sweep you up into the soul of that time, no matter how removed it is from your present reality.

When you read assigned novels for college classes, keep in mind that in expressing their times, they can help you understand why people living in that era behaved as they did—and that they might not be very different from you and people you know. Plus, immersing yourself in the past, or in another culture, can allow you to see your own everyday surroundings more sharply and perhaps more critically.

Look for novels like the following when you want to experience the flavor and texture of another world, one that is totally different yet strangely familiar to your own. The combination of freedom and emptiness for the young Lost Generation surviving World War I is perfectly captured in Ernest Hemingway's *The Sun Also Rises* (1926). In novels like *The Great Gatsby* (1925) and *The Last Tycoon* (1941), F. Scott Fitzgerald recreates the sparkle and superficiality of the 1920s Jazz Age, an era of high spirits and lawlessness that you may have also seen dramatized in the movie *Chicago*.

John Steinbeck's *The Grapes of Wrath* (1939) captures the stubborn toughness and surprising tenderness of the Oklahoma Dust Bowl immigrants of the 1930s. In Jack Kerouac's *On the Road* (1957), readers of any age can groove to the cool pulse of the 1950s Beat Generation. To understand better what it must have been like to be African American in the twentieth century, sample the novels of Ralph Ellison, James Baldwin, or Zora Neale Hurston. To appreciate what it meant to be Jewish in the United States during the same era, check out the novels of Saul Bellow, Bernard Malamud, or Philip Roth.

For many people, the best way to grasp a moment in history is through a personal account. A letter home written by a soldier in Vietnam might say more about that time than any documentary or history book. In the same way, fiction can show us a snapshot of a past or present culture, lifestyle, or society with the vivid immediacy of detail that a nonfiction chronicle could never match. The trick to reading the novel as an expression of its times is to let go of your prior knowledge and allow yourself to identify with the era, however distant or far away.

So, novels, just like the violent and heroic epics of old, have the power to hypnotize us, move us, and help us celebrate our struggles to surmount obstacles in life. If you appreciate a good story, and we all do, a novel will deliver in a way that can give you a new take on problems, an escape from dull routine, a radical viewpoint on a political issue, or an impression of a time or a culture that will drop you into the middle of a startling new reality. Novels are tools for changing your world. Use them!

Putting this chapter to work

Apply this chapter to the novel you are reading by asking yourself the following questions:

- If this novel were a mirror, what image of life would I see reflected in it?
- What is there about this novel that could be called *epic*?

- What questions does the narrative stir up in my mind?
- Of the four uses of the novel in this chapter, which would I say best fits this novel? How so?
- In what ways could reading this novel benefit the reader?

2

How Novels Work

In this chapter, you will:

- Identify the elements that novels are built from
- Understand how those elements affect the novel's structure
- Relate elements of the novel to other genres, such as film
- Discover signals for recognizing those elements in the novel you are reading

A novel is made up of components working together to propel a story forward, in the same way that a car engine's moving parts make it hum and accelerate. Instinctively, readers sense the presence of the various elements, like plot and characterization, that drive a narrative.

In college, you can expect to learn about the terms for a novel's elements. You will recognize many of them, either from reading or from talking about movies: "The plot dragged in the second half," or "I loved the character of Juno." Identifying these elements will give you an insider's perspective on how an author has designed his or her vehicle and what you can expect the ride to be like.

Premise

Reading a novel is like signing a contract. Readers agree to enter a novel's world without hesitation—but only if they understand its ground rules. These ground rules are known as the novel's premise, meaning something that is assumed or taken for granted.

For example, in the world of Mary Shelley's novel *Frankenstein*, Shelley sets up the supernatural premise that it is possible for a scientist to create a living creature from decaying flesh. Readers who buy this gruesome premise—and there have been millions of satisfied customers—will also believe in all the dread and horror and guilt resulting from it as the narrative unfolds.

When readers accept a supernatural premise like Shelley's, they are entering into a deal with the author that poet Samuel Taylor Coleridge called "the willing suspension of disbelief." But even realistic fiction asks its readers to take a leap of faith and just believe.

From the start, a good novelist clues us in about his or her premise. Is the novel's world supposed to work like the everyday world? Or does it work according to some other set of rules—entering the troubled mind of a paranoid character, as in the character of Lenny in the 2000 psychological thriller film *Memento*. Lenny tries to show us reality as he understands it, but his grip on real life is questionable.

Readers expect a novel to meet the expectations set up by its premise. A nonexperimental novel consistently follows the ground rules it sets up. By contrast, an experimental novel breaks its own rules at random, sometimes at the risk of turning off a reader who is expecting order and predictability.

When you read to discover the premise, try asking yourself questions like the following:

- Is the author laying out any ground rules that I am being asked to accept before going forward? (For example, the idea that people can be created and manipulated in test tubes, as in *Brave New World*.)
- Can the idea of the story be expressed as a "What if" question? (For example, what if a vampire and a human girl fell in love, as in *Twilight*?)
- How would I translate the premise of the novel into my own words?
- Is the novel's premise realistic, or is it fantasy?
- Why did the author choose this particular premise? How does it make it easier for the novelist to get his or her point across?

Setting

After the novel's premise has been established and author and reader have entered into a silent partnership, how does the novelist go about constructing his or her created world? What are the basic materials of fiction? Setting is one of a novel's most important elements.

If you have just seen the movie *Flags of Our Fathers*, a friend who doesn't know the film might ask you, "What was the setting?" You could say, "The sacred Japanese island of Iwo Jima," or "World War II," or "A bloody battle." All of your answers would be correct. A setting includes location, time, and anything else that sets the context in which a story takes place. A story's context—the environment or situation surrounding the events—can mean the society or culture in which the narrative unfolds, the geographical area, the historical period, or even the season of the year.

A novel's setting can be the first thing that appeals to an audience. Some readers might be drawn to Joseph Conrad or Herman Melville simply because their works depict life at sea. Later, after being hooked by the nautical settings, the same readers end up appreciating the tangled human relationships these novelists explore.

A novel can spotlight a setting that is so interesting or authentic or beautiful that readers think of it as a character they know and love. For example, in *Wuthering Heights* (1847), Emily Brontë's descriptions of the lonesome, windswept moors (expanses of open, rolling land) loom large in the minds of her readers—loyal fans trek to Yorkshire just to see them up close.

Settings can be imaginary (think Hogwarts, Middle Earth, or the futuristic world of George Orwell's *1984*). Or they can be fictional versions of real places (for example, Smallville and Metropolis in the TV series *Smallville*). Regardless of their basis in fact, fictional settings are successful when they craft a convincing environment for their characters to live in.

In addition to creating a workable world, setting can suggest why characters behave the way they do. For example, the award-winning HBO fantasy television series *A Game of Thrones* is set in the Seven Kingdoms of Westeros, as well as in an ice-covered region north of Westeros and an eastern continent across a narrow sea. The geographical limitations of this world give the warring noble families something to fight about, and that, in turn, reveals how people in power can use or abuse that power.

When you read to focus on setting, ask yourself questions like these:

- Is the setting imaginary? If so, do I think it is similar to real life in any way? What about the imaginary setting is different from real life?
- Is the novel set in the future? What elements of the setting show me that the setting is futuristic?
- Does the setting play a part in the way characters act? If the setting were different, do I think the characters would behave differently?
- Does the setting strike me as dramatic? In what way? Is it distracting or does it add to my enjoyment of the novel?
- Is the setting meant to be realistic? If I am familiar with the real-life place, do I buy the author's version of it?
- How does the setting make me feel?
- What is the major element of this novel's setting: for example, an isolated town, a crowded city, a drifting boat, an upscale neighborhood, a competitive school? Does it work for me?

Plot

A plot is like the step-by-step driving directions you print from a search engine. It's a plan of turns, stoplights, and freeway ramps that the author follows to get his characters from one place to another in the story. A novel's plot might navigate a boy from a small town in Missouri through a series of adventures on a river raft and then back again, as in the case of Mark Twain's classic novel *The Adventures of Huckleberry Finn* (1885).

But a novel's plot is not just a navigation system in the ordinary sense of getting a vehicle from here to there in time and space. It's also a plan for an author's characters to arrive at new viewpoints or dead ends in their journey of self-discovery throughout the story.

In the case of Twain's novel, Huck returns from his adventures changed because he realizes the humanity of the slave, Jim, and comes to see slavery as a cruel and unjust institution, something he didn't recognize at the beginning of the novel. Twain's plot allows Huck to arrive at this new mental outlook, and it takes the reader there too, in a way that mere lecturing never would.

A novel's plot depends on conflict. The blow-by-blow account of the conflict and how—or if—it is resolved forms the backbone of the plot. The protagonist, or main character, is in conflict with some antagonist. (The root *agon* is Greek for "contest.")

The antagonist is usually another character, but need not be. A force of nature, a challenging choice, an entire group of people, or the character's own mind can all be antagonists. The way in which the protagonist fights the antagonist determines important plot twists and turns.

Usually, unless the novel is experimental, the events of a novel's plot follow an orderly progression of cause and effect: First some event happens; because of it, the next event happens, and so on. Usually the progression is chronological, but as with many movies, a novel can present events out of time order, using the devices we think of as cinematic, like flashback and flash forward.

For example, the 2004 movie *Eternal Sunshine of the Spotless Mind*, about a company that erases people's memories, jumps back and forth in time. So much so, in fact, that viewers pay attention to the character Clementine's hair color—which morphs from tangerine to green to blue—in order to keep track of time.

Whichever way a novelist chooses to unwind a plot, he or she is expected to include tension in the form of suspense: Will Jane Eyre eventually marry Mr. Rochester? Will the protagonist of *Crime and Punishment* eventually be punished for his crime? Will Celie in *The Color Purple* eventually become financially and emotionally independent? If a novel's plot lacks suspense, it loses its grip on the audience.

A good plot doesn't have to be original—it can borrow from real life. The plot of Sylvia Plath's 1963 novel *The Bell Jar* is based on her real-life breakdown while working as a young magazine intern in New York City. And the plot of the 2010 movie *The Social Network* is based on the events surrounding the creation of Facebook. When you read a novel with a plot based on real-life events, consider what makes the situation so compelling that the author would want to recreate it.

When you read to discover plot, try asking yourself questions like these:

- What is the major conflict or struggle?
- Who is the protagonist? Who or what is the antagonist?
- Is the story told in chronological order, or in an usual order using special devices like flashbacks?
- Where is the suspense in the plot? What creates this tension?
- Is the plot fictional, or is it based on real-life events?

Characters and dialogue

Without characters acting and reacting to events, a novel has no story. Like real human beings, characters have good and bad traits, dreams and schemes. And in a novel, characters face problems. Whether the trouble stems from their own faults or from circumstances beyond their control—from indecisiveness or overconfidence, or from misunderstandings or unforeseen events—the characters' growth, or lack of it, in response to crisis makes a story that readers either care about deeply or not at all.

As long as they move the reader, characters can be human or inhuman, single or various. In Jack London's *White Fang* (1906), one of the central characters is a wolf-dog hybrid; in Orwell's *Animal Farm* (1945), the villains are pigs.

In Russian novels, such as Leo Tolstoy's 1869 epic *War and Peace* (one of the longest novels ever written), the reader must keep track of dozens of characters, all with tongue-twister names like Mikhail Ilarionovich Kutuzov and Andrei Nikolayevich Bolkonsky. Any of Tolstoy's individual characters, however, is less important than the social group he or she belongs to, which is like a character in itself.

Speaking of character names, some authors choose names that reveal something about the people who populate their book or about the book's plot. In her 1984 novel *The House on Mango Street*, for instance, Sandra Cisneros gives her main character the name Esperanza, which means "hope" in Spanish. And in Nathaniel Hawthorne's 1850 classic *The Scarlet Letter*, much discussion has centered on what the name of a mysterious little girl, Pearl, could possibly mean.

Whether you read a novel on your own or for a college assignment, notice the dialogue. What does a character say, and what do others say *about* him or her? Novelists use dialogue to show what type of people the characters are, what they are thinking and feeling, and what motivates them. For example, in *Animal Farm,* when the pigs who rule the farm issue the illogical statement: "All animals are equal, but some animals are more equal than others," Orwell is commenting on the hypocrisy of the pigs, who pretend to treat all citizens equally but then try to justify their own unfair actions in giving privileges to a small, elite group of animals. And when Dr. Frankenstein says, "The world was to me a secret which I desired to divine," you should probably consider yourself warned of nail-biting events to come.

Playwrights since the time of Shakespeare have used the soliloquy, an actor alone on stage speaking thoughts aloud. Similarly, novelists frequently write interior monologues, allowing the reader to overhear a character's private musings. When you are reading an interior monologue to discover the motivation of a character, take such information with a grain of salt: Sometimes characters reveal themselves most completely by what the author has them keep silent about, even when talking to themselves.

When you read to discover characterization, try asking yourself questions like the following:

- What are the characters' social classes or types of backgrounds?
- Who is the main character or protagonist?
- What does the character want? In other words, what makes him or her tick?
- Does the character's name have any hidden meaning?
- What does a given character say about him or herself? What do others say about the character? Is there a difference? Why?
- Can you list the traits (dishonesty, courage, shyness, and so on) of a particular character?
- Does the character grow or change by the end of the novel? How and why?

Narrative mode or point of view

In ancient times, epic stories were told—or more likely sung—by a narrator who commented on the action of the story, telling the audience exactly what their opinions should be. The ancient Greeks used the chorus in their comedies and tragedies, a gathering of anonymous characters on stage who piped up with background information and summaries that helped the audience understand the play. But this sort of intrusive narration tended to get in the way of a story feeling real because the audience was always being distracted from the main action.

Over the centuries, novelists have played with various ways of making sure that their audience follows the thread of the story, while at the same time maintaining the illusion that their characters are unpredictable and conflicted living beings who are likely to do just about anything.

Point of view refers to the lens, or perspective, through which readers watch the action unfold. In life and in fiction, point of view can change the way we interpret events. A traffic accident or a domestic squabble is going to sound different depending on who's telling the story.

In novels, the most common narrative mode, or way of telling a story, is the third-person point of view. There are two types of third-person point of view.

In the first, omniscient (all-knowing), the voice telling the story presents the inner thoughts and feelings of every character. This means that a third-person omniscient narrator knows that Robert is planning to murder Gwendolyn with a toothpick. But he also knows that Gwendolyn is on to Robert and plans to slay him with a paper clip. In this third-person omniscient scenario, the narrator also knows that neither Robert nor Gwendolyn is aware of the homicidal urges of the other. The readers, on the other hand, know everything because the third-person omniscient narrator tells them about it. Usually, the omniscient narrator is not present as a character, but is a stand-in for the writer, talking directly to the reader.

The second type of third-person point of view is called limited because the point of view is limited to just one character who participates in the action. For example, in J. K. Rowling's *Harry Potter* series, the reader sees everything through Harry Potter's eyes and cannot know anything Harry himself doesn't know.

Less common than third-person and much more tricky to interpret is the first-person narrative mode. The first-person narrator is a character who is part of the action, but may not be the main character. Fitzgerald's 1925 novel *The Great Gatsby*, for example, isn't narrated by Gatsby himself, but by a minor character, Nick Carraway. Because the narrator is part of the developing story, he or she may or may not know all the juicy details of what's going on.

Because first-person narrators can't show readers everything about ongoing events, we can't always count on them to be accurate, or even reliable. In fact, novelists sometimes deliberately use an unreliable narrator to make things interesting and reveal a truth about human nature. An unreliable narrator might be crazy, a liar, or unable to accept the real truth.

For example, in *The Remains of the Day* (1989) by Kazuo Ishiguro, an aging butler, Stevens, is the first-person narrator. As he looks back on his past to reassure himself that the employer he devoted his life to really was a great man, he unknowingly reveals to us his own self-deception. By the time Stevens realizes what a fool he has been to give up the love of a fine woman merely to serve an unworthy master, the reader has already gotten there ahead of him.

Furthermore, as readers become aware of Stevens's pathetic attempts to delude himself, the dramatic irony of the situation grows. Dramatic irony occurs when a reader knows something that a character doesn't—and possibly pities that character.

Novels written in the first-person narrative mode can give readers a chance to get inside the head of the character who narrates. If a novelist creates a unique voice, readers may continue to hear echoes of the way that character speaks and thinks even after they close the book.

When you read to discover narrative mode or point of view, try asking yourself questions like the following:

- What "person" is the story told from: first person, third-person omniscient, third-person limited? How can I tell?
- Through whose eyes is the story told?
- If it is a first-person viewpoint, can that person be trusted? Do I like that person?
- Is the story told from multiple viewpoints? How does that help the story?
- Does the character telling the story have a unique way of talking? What is it? Does it distract me from the story or add to my enjoyment of it?

Theme

Being asked to identify the theme of a work of fiction is often frustrating for students. You wish that a novel's theme could be a clear-cut message from author to reader. You feel like you should be able find the theme clearly stated somewhere in the text of the story. But it isn't that straightforward; if it were, the author would write a sermon, a greeting card, or an instruction manual, not a novel.

It helps to think of the word *theme* as it is used when talking about music. In a piece of music, a theme is a repeated melody. It comes up over and over again, sometimes varied in tempo or key, but always recognizable, always seeming to communicate without words the essential emotional quality of the music. The melody that fills the soundtracks of movies is often called theme music. So a theme in this sense means a repeated musical element or idea that runs through an entire work.

You can also think about theme this way: In classrooms of the recent past, teachers assigned students to write papers called themes. A theme was a written exercise with a distinct and unifying idea. So you can think of a novel's theme as a repeated idea that runs through the novel, or as a single, overarching thought that ties it all together.

As a reader and an intelligent human being, you have your own take on the ideas an author weaves into his or her novels. So ask yourself questions like the following when you read to discover theme:

- What does this mean?
- Why does the author bring it up?
- What ideas does it suggest?
- Why is it important?

Novels usually have multiple themes. The following lists show you the range of possibilities when you read for theme.

Themes from Amy Tan's 1989 novel *The Joy Luck Club*:
- Women's changing roles
- The American dream and immigrants

- The limitations of language
- Sacrificing for family

Themes from Jennifer Egan's 2010 novel *A Visit from the Goon Squad*:
- Aging as a robber of youth, innocence, and success
- Memory
- Dealing with change

Themes from Jonathan Franzen's 2010 novel *Freedom*:
- Nature versus materialism
- The freedom to suffer
- Depression
- Corporate hypocrisy
- Families and their faults

Themes from Virginia Woolf's 1925 novel *Mrs. Dalloway*:
- Disappointment with the British Empire
- Fear of death
- Communication versus privacy
- Social pressure to conform

Themes from J. D. Salinger's 1951 novel *Catcher in the Rye*:
- Alienation and loneliness
- The pain of maturing
- Adulthood as false and phony
- Relationships and sexuality

Symbolism

A symbol is a sign that packs much meaning into a simple image: A skull and crossbones symbol on a bottle of drain cleaner means pain, agony, and death for any person who swallows it. For warring gang members, a red or a blue article of clothing might mean the difference between enemy and ally. A simple flag can represent an entire beloved or hated nation.

When you read, watch for symbols, images that are more than what they appear to be. For example, in a 1904 novel by Henry

James, *The Golden Bowl,* a shattered bowl represents the death of a relationship in a way that makes that abstract breakup an actual object, wrecked beyond repair, that the novel's characters, and you the reader, can almost touch.

Often, symbols in fiction are not trumpeted as meaning anything special; they are just part of the fabric of the story. For example, the green light across the water that Jay Gatsby stares at longingly in Fitzgerald's novel stands for all of Gatsby's hopes and dreams, close enough to tantalize yet never close enough to touch. But the green light is also an ordinary part of the skyline. It's up to you—with some hints from the author—to notice its deeper meaning.

A symbol can be an action a character performs, as well. In Miguel de Cervantes's 1604 novel *Don Quixote,* the so-called ingenious knight never fails to charge forward with his lance held at the ready whenever he sees a harmless windmill, imagining himself to be fighting a giant.

This crazy act has come to represent the pointlessness of attacking imaginary enemies, or fighting unwinnable battles. In the novel, the battles are unwinnable and perhaps meaningless, but Don Quixote keeps fighting anyway and readers can't help but admire him for it. In a larger sense, his actions express the novel's theme—that it is tragic to be an idealist in a hostile world. The Don's symbolic struggle has entered the English language as the saying "tilting at windmills."

When you read to discover symbols, try asking yourself questions like the following:

- Does the author include any sort of unusual image (such as the billboard with the image of the eyeglasses in *The Great Gatsby*) that might be a symbol?
- If so, what idea do I think the symbol stands for?
- Does the title of the novel contain a symbol that I can decode?
- Is there any everyday object in the novel that might be a symbol in disguise?
- Is there any mention of a descriptive detail, such as color, that might stand for something? (Red for love, for example?)

- Does the author use any names or expressions that might be symbolic? For example, the Valley of Ashes in *The Great Gatsby*, which might stand for the all-consuming consequences of greed?
- Is there any particular condition or situation (blindness, pregnancy) that might have a symbolic meaning?
- Is there any element of nature in the novel, such as the ocean, a mountain, or a type of animal, that might be symbolic?

So, novels use a range of different tools to construct meaning. As the reader, you have tools, too: life experience, an understanding of human nature, and the ability to put two and two together. When you read a novel you become part of the game of meaning-making. Your strategy as you play will make or break the outcome, turning the simple act of page turning while scanning with your eyes into an experience that will rock you.

Putting this chapter to work

Apply this chapter to the novel you are reading by asking yourself the following questions:

- How does a certain element (characterization, for example) help propel this novel forward and make me want to keep reading?
- Is the premise of this novel hard to swallow? If it is hard to suspend disbelief, why does the author want me to do so? Why didn't the author choose a more believable premise?
- Do I identify with the viewpoint the novel's story is told from? Why or why not? Does this interfere with the author's message?
- Have I seen a movie version of this novel? How are the two alike and different?
- Do I plan to discuss this novel with others reading it? If so, can I come up with some questions for discussion ahead of time?
- Is there any event in the novel I find hard to understand (such as the ending of *The Awakening*)? If so, could it possibly be symbolic of something? Of what?

3

Recognize Types of Novels

In this chapter, you will:

- Recognize the meaning of the term *genre* as applied to novels
- Identify the common novel genres
- Understand why novelists choose particular genres
- Discover signs that point to the genre of the novel you are reading

Your MP3 player sorts your music collection by genre: hip hop, pop, country. Your friend on Facebook lists her favorite movie genres as action, comedy, and fantasy. In the same way, novels are categorized by type. Genre means a category of artistic work, characterized by a definitely identifiable style.

As with music or movies, your favorite novel genres reveal something about your interests and inclinations. You can be attracted to certain genres based on personal taste, familiarity, or a desire to experience something new. A seasoned novel reader settles into a hot bath with a vintage Agatha Christie detective novel to relax, but dives into an exciting *Harry Potter* adventure to be swept into a world of sword and sorcery.

In addition to guiding your choices when reading for pleasure, knowing the different types of novel helps you set your expectations when you read for a college assignment. You wouldn't approach *The Big Sleep* in the same way you would *The Awakening*.

Romantic novels

Throughout history, movements—many people joining to achieve change—have sparked new genres of art, music, and literature. Romanticism was a stormy movement of Western civilization stretching from the late eighteenth century to the mid-nineteenth century. Romantics rejected order, harmony, and tranquility in favor of spontaneity, rebellion, and passion.

The Sorrows of Young Werther by Johann Wolfgang von Goethe was one of the earliest novels of the romantic literary movement. First published in 1774, it tells of a young artist, Werther, who falls in love with a beautiful young woman, Lotte. Even after Lotte marries an older man, Werther can't move on. Lotte decides that she and Werther should never see each other again. Despairing, he shoots himself.

Although Werther is obsessed with Lotte, his true obsession is with own feelings. In his first-person narrative, he relives his desire and misery in intense detail. Goethe's focus on the tortured emotions of Werther paved the way for later romantic novels.

A powerful later romantic novel is *Wuthering Heights* (1847) by Emily Brontë. Catherine, a dramatic, stubborn, self-centered young woman, loses her heart and soul to Heathcliff, a fierce and passionate lover who turns cruel and bitter after she rejects him to marry a rich admirer.

Heathcliff is such an explosive character that even the author's own sister (Charlotte Brontë, author of another classic, *Jane Eyre*) wrote in an introduction to the book that perhaps authors shouldn't upset their readers by dreaming up disturbing characters like Heathcliff.

Popular novels described as romantic, such as the *Twilight* Series or *The Notebook* (1996), also deal with out-of-control emotions and magnetic physical and spiritual attraction between lovers. The genre is still alive and kicking, but many critics think the best romantic novels are the old ones.

Realistic novels

Not every artist of the nineteenth century was attracted to romanticism. Many authors rejected the qualities of tenderness, idealism, and passionate love as nonsense. The novels of Stendhal and Honoré de Balzac, for example, swung to the opposite extreme, representing life as grim and most people as vicious and animal-like. And in 1967, S. E. Hinton spared her readers none of the ugly details of gang rivalry, bullying, and suicide in *The Outsiders.*

In the twentieth century, war novels were likely to be harsh and shocking in their descriptions of battle scenes. Erich Maria Remarque's *All Quiet on the Western Front* (1929) is an example. But contemporary realistic novels, although they can be dark and bitter, can also include hope for reforming the degraded human conditions they describe.

Naturalistic novels

Naturalism, a literary movement that started in the late nineteenth century, was an outgrowth of realism. The novelist describes characters and situations as imperfect products of an indifferent universe, rather than as prettied up, idealized beings. The author might describe the bodily functions of his characters, or deal frankly with their sexuality. Émile Zola was an early naturalistic writer.

Naturalists, influenced by the new scientific thought of Charles Darwin, tried to show in their work that people are part of nature, not superior to it. Whereas realists tried to show people as they are, naturalists tried to prove that they act that way because of forces of nature, such as the environment or heredity.

Naturalistic novelists often treated their characters as specimens to be scientifically examined. For example, when the novelist Stephen Crane wrote *Maggie: A Girl of the Streets* in 1893, he shadowed female prostitutes, taking notes and copying their street slang. *An American Tragedy* (1925) by Theodore Dreiser is a naturalistic novel that dissects, like a television docudrama, a real-life criminal case.

Naturalism was most popular between 1890 and 1925, but later novelists were influenced by it. Ernest Hemingway's work (think *The Old Man and the Sea*) often shows individuals in conflict with their hostile natural environments. Sherwood Anderson (1876–1941) and Sinclair Lewis (1885–1951) also used the naturalistic method of analyzing characters, almost as though they were lab rats in a scientific study.

Avant-garde novels

Fiction categorized as avant-garde—meaning cutting edge, or ahead of the pack (French, "advance guard")—develops new or experimental methods of storytelling. A rush of avant-garde novels were written in the years following World War I. Beginning in France and spreading the world over, avant-garde novels were a response to the horrors, often kept secret by governments, of modern scientific warfare. Challenging the old patriotism with a new outrageousness and irreverence, novelists played with new ways to narrate.

For example, James Joyce's *Finnegan's Wake* (1939) begins with the end of a sentence left unfinished on the last page. It's filled with multiple languages and made-up words. Characters from literature and history exit and enter seemingly at random. Joyce's novel is challenging, but it creates a unique dreamlike atmosphere that its readers have found amazing.

Often, readers are part of the process of creation in avant-garde novels. In an experimental novel by Vladimir Nabokov, *Pale Fire* (1962), the reader pieces together events via the author's presentation of a 999-line poem and a fictional critique of that poem apparently written by an insane man. In *Hopscotch* (1966), by the Argentine writer Julio Cortázar, the reader must work to make sense of multiple narrators and optional endings.

Hopscotch, like many other experimental novels, features a stream-of-consciousness narrative method. Stream of consciousness is a form of interior monologue in which a character's thoughts are written as they would sound if they were being overhead—disjointed, fragmented, ungrammatical, and illogical. Again, this type of novel asks readers to make sense of the narrative but at the same time surrender to the flood of words.

Many contemporary novels use narrative techniques that were once considered avant-garde. For example, in *A Visit From the Goon Squad* (2010), Jennifer Egan experiments with alternative forms of narration, including telling a segment of the story through a mock PowerPoint presentation. Mark Haddon's *The Curious Incident of the Dog in the Night-Time* (2003) is told from the viewpoint of a teen boy with a condition similar to autism or Asperger's syndrome. In *Infinite Jest* (1996), David Foster Wallace interrupts the flow of his novel with endnotes to shatter the expected structure of the narrative. Again, the reader participates in making sense out of these storytelling techniques.

Gothic novels

The term *gothic* refers to a style of fiction that chooses spooky and isolated locales, such as a decaying castle or haunted mansion, as the settings for weird, mysterious, or violent events.

One of the first gothic novels was Horace Walpole's *Castle of Otranto* (1765), which involves mysterious deaths (one man is flattened by a falling helmet) and people locking one another in towers. Mary Shelley's *Frankenstein*, with its notorious monster, is another famous gothic novel. By the later eighteenth century, the gothic genre was so popular that Jane Austen poked fun at it with her satiric gothic novel *Northanger Abbey* (1817).

In the twentieth century, writers like Daphne DuMaurier and Stephen King continued the gothic tradition. The genre is still popular today, especially in vampire novels, such as Stephenie Meyer's *Twilight* series, which have their origins in Bram Stoker's *Dracula* (1897).

Although gothic novels stir up emotions like terror and pity, readers don't take this sort of fiction as seriously as they would a genre like realism. Instead, people read gothic novels for the thrills and chills, and they admire the authors who can stimulate those temporary reactions with style and finesse. Even so, a gothic novel like *Frankenstein* can raise serious questions about human psychology.

Coming-of-age novels

The coming-of-age novel—also known as the bildungsroman, from the German for "formation" plus "novel"—tells the story of a young person's development or spiritual education. The coming-of-age novel is one of the easiest types of novels to identify with because we have all experienced the challenges and adventures of growing up.

Many classic coming-of-age novels show the growing pains of their characters as they come to grips with cruelty in the world. Other young characters are shown becoming stronger as they face various challenges.

The meaningful themes and lasting appeal of the coming-of-age novel speak for themselves. Following is a short list of old and new classics in the genre:

- *The Adventures of Huckleberry Finn* by Mark Twain
- *Catcher in the Rye* by J. D. Salinger
- *The Color Purple* by Alice Walker
- *Great Expectations* by Charles Dickens
- *The House on Mango Street* by Sandra Cisneros
- *The Kite Runner* by Khaled Hosseini
- *Never Let Me Go* by Kazuo Ishiguro
- *A Portrait of the Artist as a Young Man* by James Joyce
- *A Separate Peace* by John Knowles
- *Siddhartha* by Hermann Hesse
- *Song of Solomon* by Toni Morrison
- *To Kill a Mockingbird* by Harper Lee
- *A Tree Grows in Brooklyn* by Betty Smith

Detective novels

Given that at least three different versions of the popular television show *Law and Order* are broadcast on any given day, it's clear that the detective story—also known as the crime novel, mystery, or thriller—has lasting appeal as entertainment. Novelists of this genre have shocked our sensibilities and puzzled our minds for generations.

Although they are often considered lightweight reading, good detective novels are challenging to write, requiring skillful plotting, the ability to maintain suspense, and the ability to write concisely. Readers experience the unfolding of the carefully crafted mystery through the eyes of the main character. These are typically brilliant but eccentric private investigators, attorneys, or police officers. Sherlock Holmes, the hero of Sir Arthur Conan Doyle's series of novels, is a classic example.

Edgar Allan Poe, the poet and fiction writer whose short stories are associated with the gothic genre, is credited with starting the detective novel tradition with his short story "Murders in the Rue Morgue" (1841). His characters, like Sherlock Holmes, use ratiocination, the process of exact reasoning, to think their way toward solutions to mysteries.

In the 1860s, Wilkie Collins followed in Poe's footsteps, writing *Moonstone* and *Woman in White*. *Woman in White*, serialized in 1859 and published in book form in 1860, was inspired by an actual criminal case and is considered by some critics to be the world's first mystery novel. Downloaded on e-readers, its popularity endures today.

Contemporary writers in the detective novel genre and some of their famous protagonists include Mickey Spillane (Mike Hammer), Dashiell Hammett (Sam Spade), Agatha Christie (Hercule Poirot), Dorothy L. Sayers (Lord Peter Wimsey), Sue Grafton (Kinsey Millhone), and Stieg Larsson (Lisbeth Salander).

Western novels

An idea known as the frontier myth is central to all novels about the early American West. The desire to "boldly go where no man has gone before," as the television and movie series *Star Trek* puts it, is a recurring fascination of humankind. On the one hand, people seem to have an inborn instinct to tame what is wild. On the other hand, people are also tempted to escape from civilization and revel in lawlessness. The tension between civilization and anarchy (when anything goes) is the attraction of the western novel.

Early nineteenth-century adventure novels of the American wilderness, like James Fenimore Cooper's *Last of the Mohicans* (1826), were the forerunners of the western genre. But it was author Zane Grey (1872–1939) who developed it into a legacy, penning more than eighty western novels, of which *Riders of the Purple Sage* (1912) was the most popular.

Western novels can be pure entertainment, but they can also be serious fiction. Larry McMurtry won the 1986 Pulitzer Prize for Fiction with *Lonesome Dove* (1985), about relationships between Texas Rangers who drive a cattle herd from Texas to Montana. The tale is loosely based on the adventures of real-life cattle drivers Oliver Loving and Charles Goodnight, who supplied beef to the Confederacy during the Civil War.

Dystopian novels

A utopia is an ideal community. Because there is no such perfect place, it's fitting that the term *utopia* comes from the Greek words *not* and *place*, or "nowhere." Sir Thomas More's *Utopia* (1515) describes his idea of a community in which everything is governed by reason rather than by greed or self-interest. But Plato was writing about utopias well before More: His *Republic* presents his ideas for a model civilization.

An anti-utopia, or dystopia, presents a society that is repressed and controlled, often operating under the disguise of being utopian. *Brave New World* (1932) by Aldous Huxley is a dystopian novel set in the year 2540. In the World State, people are not born, but produced in hatcheries.

The developing fetuses are sorted into categories or castes, each designed to be progressively smarter than the last and destined to fill preassigned slots in society. Sex is strictly for recreation (one of the female characters is criticized by her friends for not being promiscuous enough).

John, a character who has grown up on a primitive reservation outside this dystopian world, represents the positive qualities of humankind. In the end, the corruption of the World State is too much for him.

Huxley's dystopia, as well as George Orwell's in his 1949 futuristic novel, *1984*, represents oppression and control. Huxley's themes include the abuse of technology, and people's spirituality as no match for the rapid pace of technological growth.

Relatively recent novels that offer disturbing images of the future include *A Clockwork Orange* (1962) by Anthony Burgess and *Fahrenheit 451* (1953) by Ray Bradbury. Novels such as these base their premises on extrapolation, or intelligent guessing, about what will happen based on what is currently known. In other words, dystopian authors ask themselves, and their readers, What's the worst-case scenario if we keep doing the things we do?

Specifically, *A Clockwork Orange* extrapolates (or asks What if?) about a futuristic idea of criminal control based on the existing system of crime and punishment that already existed when Burgess wrote the novel. And Bradbury extrapolates an extreme view of censorship, based on book banning in his own time.

Other types of novels

As a vehicle for spiriting people away from everyday life and carrying them to new levels of understanding, the novel deserves its longtime respect from the reading public. As a narrative form, the novel has been around long enough to develop into many more types and subcategories. The following are just a few that have emerged over the course of centuries:

- The picaresque novel
- The sentimental novel
- The novel of manners
- The epistolary novel
- The allegory

Picaresque novels

In seventeenth-century Spain, a rascal or jokester who was as likely to pick your pocket as he was to shake your hand was known as a picaro. Stories about picaros were told in the form of a series of loosely connected episodes. In this sense, Cervantes's great novel *Don Quixote* is a picaresque, or episodic, novel about the sad and funny adventures of an eccentric but oddly noble hero. John Kennedy Toole's *A Confederacy of Dunces* (1980), Rita Mae Brown's *Rubyfruit Jungle* (1973) and Aravind Adiga's *The White Tiger* (2008) are contemporary examples of the picaresque genre.

Sentimental novels

Today, the word *sentimental* usually refers to the sniffle-provoking messages of greeting cards or advertisements. In the 1700s, however, sentiment referred to refined and elevated feelings. Samuel Richardson's classic novel *Pamela, or Virtue Rewarded* (1740) claimed that passionate attraction between men and women could rise above mere physicality and exist as pure sentiment.

Novels of manners

A novel of manners ("manners" in the sense of the ways things are done) creates a complex social world for the reader, showing in detail the beliefs, customs, and values of its members. Characters are measured according to how well they live up to the requirements of their society. Jane Austen was masterful at the novel of manners. Other authors of this genre include Henry James, Evelyn Waugh, and Edith Wharton.

Epistolary novels

An epistle is a letter. The term *epistolary novel*, then, describes not so much a genre as a method of telling a story. The technique is an old one. Aphra Behn's *Love-Letters Between a Nobleman and His Sister* (1684) is considered one of the first epistolary novels. The development of plot through a series of letters is common to all genres: Richardson's sentimental novel *Pamela* unfolds via letters written by the beautiful young serving maid to her parents; the coming-of-age novel *The Color Purple* unfolds via letters written by Celie to God.

Allegories

Even today, authors make use of the age-old device of allegory, which means a fictional story that communicates its hidden meaning through symbolic figures or events. John Bunyan's *The Pilgrim's Progress* (1678), an early allegory, tells the story of a Christian man's developing faith. The spiritual journey is told as if it were a real journey. An extremely popular modern allegory, Paolo Coelho's *The Alchemist* (1988) is also about a spiritual journey. Other allegorical novels include William Golding's *Lord of the Flies*, George Orwell's *Animal Farm*, Richard Bach's *Jonathan Livingston Seagull*, and Antoine de Saint-Exupéry's *The Little Prince*.

   Modern novelists for example, Don DeLillo—frequently experiment with or combine genres. But if you know something about a novel's genre before you start reading, you will know more about what to expect from the book. Comparing different examples of the same genre—for example, reading two or three dystopian or coming-of-age novels one after the other—helps you set standards for what you think works best about that genre and why.

Building your opinions about genre will benefit you when a college professor assigns you to read a particular book in that genre. And it will help you make personal reading choices that will most likely entertain and enlighten you.

Putting this chapter to work

Apply this chapter to the novel you are reading by asking yourself the following questions:

- What genre is this novel? If I like this genre, what does that say about me?
- Why did the novelist choose to write in this genre? How does it help get the author's ideas across?
- What would this novel be like if it were written in a different genre? Retold as a western or as a romance, for example?
- If it is a coming-of-age novel, can I identify with the protagonist?
- If it is a dystopian novel, what is the novelist asking "What if?" about?
- If this novel were music, what genre of music would it be?
- Is this novel a successful example of its genre? How does it stack up against other novels in the same genre?
- Based on my experience reading this novel, would I be interested in reading more novels in this genre? Why or why not?

4

Respond Actively to Novels

In this chapter, you will:

- Respond actively to novels
- Learn specific steps for active reading
- Discover how to apply active reading strategies

Reading a novel is like cooking: if you want to eat a satisfying gourmet meal, you'll need to complete certain steps. But with reading, you have more choices in the way you perform those steps than you would in whipping up a savory fondue. That is, you probably don't need to read a novel slavishly from cover to cover, starting with the copyright page and ending with the colophon (the blurb that talks about the history of the type font chosen by the book designer). But it helps to have a plan, or you might miss something juicy.

Once, for example, as a much younger, less experienced reader, I skipped the fictional afterword to Agatha Christie's mystery, *And Then There Were None*. This afterword is written in a dry and rather pompous way from the point of view of one of the main characters, following a string of unsolved murders. (Spoiler alert: everybody on the island dies.) Compared to all the action and suspense that had come before, the afterword just looked boring and uncalled-for.

Little did I know, however, when I decided to close the book without reading this final segment, that it actually contained the character's confession to the serial massacre and how he'd done it. It was like fast-forwarding through a movie and missing the best part.

This chapter suggests steps for an *active reading plan*. When you plan to reach a goal, from getting to class on time or going on a date, you play an active role in how you get there. In the same way, when you plan your approach to reading a novel, you guarantee that you'll take an active part in the experience and make it your own.

A key factor in active reading is responding to what you read, almost as if you were talking back to the novelist or the characters themselves. Here's how to respond actively to a novel:

- Preview it for coming attractions.
- Mark it up.
- Journal about it.
- Talk about it.
- Take a second look at it.

Previewing a novel

A novel's cover is no different from the cover of a CD or DVD. You read it to get an idea of what's inside. You might feel eager—or pressured by a looming assignment deadline—to plunge into reading the actual novel. But wait. Read its front and back covers first.

You'll find clues here about what to expect. Many publishers clearly label a novel's genre, "mystery," for example. Publishers also give you a capsule summary of the book's plot, avoiding spoilers, of course. And you'll usually find quotations from other novelists or book reviewers who have already read the novel and, invariably, loved it.

Don't let what you find on a book's covers influence you one way or the other; just take it in. You'll decide for yourself whether you agree after you finish the book. But a novel's covers will always offer hints about what's in store for you as you read.

After you preview the cover, glance at the table of contents, if there is one. Do the chapter titles suggest anything about what's to come? Do they tip you off to the novel's structure? Is it conventional or experimental? Are there multiple viewpoints or just one? Are there any switches in time and place?

If there is an introduction, read it. Often written by another author or a literary critic, a novel's introduction will give you clues to cultural context. Will this be a novel of the Vietnam War era? Or is it a chronicle of life in a small Southern town in the 1950s? Was the author a participant or an outsider? You'll step into a novel's new territory with more confidence if you read its introduction first.

Additionally, the introduction will often give you a sense of how a novel's past readers have understood it. Was the novel popular when it first came out? Is it considered a success at provoking outrage at injustice? Or painting a picture of a dark possible future? Or shedding light on what it's like to be in a certain group? How does it match up against other novels of its genre? You'll often find this kind of insider information here.

Finally, preview the novel's length and complexity. As a college reader, you are reading against time, scheduling your completion of the novel in conjunction with your professor's timetable and your assignments in other courses.

That paperback on your bedside table might look skinny, but its font might be small and dense, making it longer than you think. How long do you figure it will take to read it in accordance with your instructor's requirements? Two days? Two weeks? Two months? Regardless, plan accordingly, assigning yourself to read a certain number of pages or chapters each reading session.

And plan to read every day. Unlike a movie, which takes a few hours of your life (and sometimes, after watching a bad movie, you wish you had those two hours back), reading a novel takes a longer chunk of time. Your time spent will be rewarded, but only if you plan your reading sessions to avoid breaking the spell of the narrative. It's better to read a little bit each day than to allow several days to go by between sessions. (Don't forget to use a bookmark, sticky note, or even a candy wrapper between the pages so that you can quickly find your starting place.)

Marking up a novel

A novel is one of the few works of art or entertainment that you can deface: If the novel is your property, write in it to your heart's content. Doubtless, you have had teachers who have told you the same thing. But why?

Again, it's all part of responding actively. Taking a highlighter, ballpoint, or pencil in hand says to your subconscious mind, "Look, I'm a part of this experience. I have a voice and I plan to use it."

Also, marking up a novel helps you keep track of your journey, like monitoring your miles per gallon on a road trip. Your experience at the beginning of the novel will be disorienting; you have a whole new planet to explore, including its rules, its people, and its language.

Because this new information can be overwhelming at first, your first markings will be basic comments about what you are beginning to find out. The markings help you assimilate, or absorb, any confusing details the author throws at you about the story's action and relationships.

At this beginning stage, you'll mark up the margin in some way when you have basic questions like these: Is Jordan Baker male or female? What is kite running exactly? What does grokking involve? Will this Boo Radley person be important later in the story? Mark the name or term to help you keep track.

Later, after you've been reading the novel for a while, you will be more comfortable with the trappings of this novel planet (*novel* comes from the Latin *novella*, meaning "new"). It will be as though you were strapped into a spacecraft with a chatty alien tour guide who is slowly becoming more familiar to you. You stop focusing on her wiggling antennae or webbed feet and start thinking about how much the two of you have in common.

At this stage in your reading, some of your markings will still be assimilative, but most of your scribblings and scratchings will be *interpretive*. That is, you will find yourself marking places in the narrative that make you wonder, worry, or hope (Is Gatsby a criminal? or, Should Lotte be encouraging Werther?) and your ideas about themes and symbols (Maybe this is all about the poor versus the rich, or I think the moor stands for the loneliness of the individual).

With the current economy and the price of paper being what they are, sometimes a novel's margins will be narrow. Of course, don't try to cram your own book into the tiny margins. Try using a set of symbols that mean something to you: two checkmarks to mark a fact you want to double check, perhaps; a star next to an image you think is important; a question mark for a confusing line of dialogue; an exclamation point for a surprising event; a circle for an obvious symbol; a wavy underline for a description you particularly like.

Here are one student's sample notes:

Student annotated reading sample from Kate Chopin's *The Awakening*

Edna Pontellier could not have told why, wishing to go to the beach with Robert, she should in the first place have declined, and in the second place have followed in obedience to one of the two contradictory impulses which impelled her.

? A certain light was beginning to dawn dimly within her—the light which, showing the way, forbids it.

At that early period it served but to bewilder her. It moved her to dreams, to thoughtfulness, to the shadowy anguish which had overcome her the midnight when she had abandoned herself to tears.

★ In short, Mrs. Pontellier was beginning to realize her position in the universe as a human being, and to recognize her relations as an individual to the world within and about her. This may seem like a ponderous weight of wisdom to descend upon the soul of a young woman of twenty-eight—

Look up perhaps more wisdom than the Holy Ghost is usually pleased to vouchsafe to any woman.

I can relate! But the beginning of things, of a world especially, is necessarily vague, tangled, chaotic, and exceedingly disturbing. How few of us ever emerge from such a beginning! How many souls perish in its tumult!

Sea = freedom? The voice of the (sea) is seductive; never ceasing, whispering, clamoring, murmuring, inviting the soul to wander for a spell in abysses of solitude; to lose itself in mazes of inward contemplation.

I like this! The voice of the sea speaks to the soul. The touch of the sea is sensuous, enfolding the body in its soft, close embrace.

E-books

What if you are reading an e-text instead of a printed book? Perhaps you sent your copy of Don DeLillo's *White Noise* straight to your android phone, iPhone, or e-reader. Check out the advantages: Does the program allow you to lift segments of text and cut and paste them to a file, for example? Can you input your own words? How can you use the electronic format to your advantage?

For example, many e-readers allow you to clip and save your favorite quotes from a novel, to highlight places in the book that you want to be able to find again, and to write on the screen with a stylus just the way you would mark a page with a pen or pencil. E-readers can even organize your notes for you by keying them to their places in the text and sending them to your desktop or laptop in a neat, easy-to-read format so you won't have to shuffle through pages of notes, or puzzle over deciphering your own handwriting.

Journaling about a novel

As with markup, writing about the novel you are currently reading helps you become an active participant in the reading experience. After all, when you see a good movie, you let it wash over you and enchant you, but then you might shake your head to snap yourself back to reality and go online to Facebook, IMDb, or Rotten Tomatoes and tap out some comments about what you've just seen. This type of writing can be evaluative (I give it four out of five stars) or just expressive (It made me curious about what it was like to live in those times).

Writing about a novel as though you were blogging or journaling is similar, except that it pays to write while you are still in the midst of the experience of reading, not after you finish the novel. For one thing, your feelings about what you are reading are probably going to change as you make your way through the maze of the story. If you note down your thoughts, suspicions, and predictions about the novel as it moves forward, you are more likely to have an entertaining and profitable trip because you'll be paying closer attention to the ride.

And finally, the audience for this type of active reading is you, not a friend or an instructor, or the Internet at large. You can say whatever you want about a book in a reading journal without fear of embarrassment or being contradicted.

What kinds of entries should you make in a reading journal? You can keep running lists of comments or questions, with a page number next to them to key your observations to the text. You can ask questions about what might happen next and then try to answer them by making predictions, referring to these predictions later to see if they were valid or missed the mark. You can consider your prior knowledge about an issue or subject (plagiarism or baseball) and write down what you know about it when the topic comes up in the novel.

Some college instructors ask for a written reader response when they give reading assignments, and a reader response is fun to do on your own, too. A reader response is a brief piece of writing, a page at most. You write a short summary of what you've read, and then write a few sentences about your reactions to it. Just say what you think. Or write about how what you've just read connects to your own life.

For example, if you summarize the scene in *Catcher in the Rye* when Holden and his sister have an argument, in your final two sentences that follow this summary you could write about how the scene reminds you of a disagreement you had with a sibling. Did your argument turn out differently from Holden and Phoebe's? Did you experience similar feelings to Holden's?

Relating the novel you are reading to your own life can help you understand it more deeply. Just think of a reader response journal entry as a simple formula:

Summary + Personal Response = New Insight

If you like, get more creative in your journaling. For example, try writing an entry from the point of view of a character in the novel, adopting their speech style and worldview. It doesn't have to be the main character. If you are reading *To Kill a Mockingbird*, for example, try writing as Atticus or Dill. Getting into the heads of the characters in a novel can help you understand them better.

Talking about a novel

Book clubs whose members all read the same book and meet to discuss it are widespread these days. Sometimes whole cities get involved, as in programs like One City, One Book, and similar community reading events. When people talk to each other about a shared experience, they get ideas about it that they might not have come up with on their own. Besides, it's fun to swap impressions of a good book.

If you are reading a novel assigned by your college instructor, chances are you know other students who are reading it for the same reason. If you can arrange it, get yourself a reading partner. Meet regularly with your partner for coffee to discuss the book as you read it; or communicate by text, tweet, e-mail, instant message, or phone call if meeting in person isn't possible.

In addition to enjoying a shared experience, reading partners can help each other. Something that has you mystified might be clear to your reading partner, and vice versa. Ask your reading partner how he or she thinks the novel is going to end up, or whether they think something is an important symbol. Do you share a favorite character? Is the plot convincing to both of you, or does one of you have trouble buying it?

Perhaps you'd rather keep your reading a solitary experience. Some people feel it spoils their enjoyment of novel reading if they have to talk about it with others. Maybe that's the case with you when you read for pleasure. But keep in mind that most college professors will expect you to participate in whole class or small group discussion about a novel they have assigned for credit.

Talking about a novel with other readers outside of class will help you feel more natural when taking part in class discussions. And always remember, you have important observations to contribute. No one else will see a novel in precisely the same way you do, and that's a good thing.

If you plan to meet to discuss a novel, you can get some ideas for how to structure your conversation from typical book club discussion questions like the following. And remember, you can adapt these questions to journaling if you'd rather work on your own.

The Buddha in the Attic by Julie Otsuka:
- Why do you think this novel is told from the first-person plural ("we") point of view? Does Otsuka's choice work for you?
- How do you feel about the way the Japanese "picture brides" are treated?

- What is something you discovered about the United States from reading this novel?

Love in the Time of Cholera by Gabriel Garcia Marquez:
- What do you think the idea of cholera, a deadly disease, symbolizes in this novel?
- Florentino can't have Fermina, so he carries on a series of love affairs, told one after the other. Is this a picaresque novel, then? What's your response to Florentino's carryings-on?
- Do you think that Fermina has a good relationship with her husband?

The Sense of an Ending by Julian Barnes:
- In what way can this novel about memory be seen as a mystery?
- What kind of person is Tony Webster? Can you trust his perception of life? How do you know?
- Why do you think Tony wants to get back in touch with Veronica?

Here are some general discussion questions you can use when discussing any novel you are reading:

- What do you think of the title? What does it mean?
- Which character did you like the most ? The least? Why?
- What kind of relationships do the characters have with each other? Are these relationships believable?
- How do the characters change in the course of the story? What triggers those changes?
- If you had to choose one character in the novel who is most like you, who would that be and why?
- Did you learn something you didn't know before?
- Did anything surprise you?
- Does anything in the novel remind you of something that happened to you?
- What is the novelist's worldview according to this novel? How can you tell?
- Did your opinion about a particular subject change after reading this novel?

- What was the strongest emotion this novel evoked in you?
- Did certain parts of the novel make you feel uncomfortable? Why?
- Was there any part of the novel you had trouble understanding? Why?
- How would you rate this novel on a scale of one to five stars?
- Whose point of view is the story told from? How does this enhance or detract from the story?
- What was unique about the setting? Did it distract from or add to your enjoyment?
- What do you think the author is trying to communicate in this novel?
- Would you recommend this novel to a friend? Why or why not?
- What was the most memorable thing about this novel?
- What would you change, if anything, about this novel? Why?
- Have you read anything else by this author? How does it compare to this novel?

Take a second look at the novel

When you visit a place for the second time, whether it's a vacation destination, a new friend's home, or the pharmacy in your new neighborhood, your second visit is always informed by the first. That is, the second time around you aren't so surprised by that velvet painting of the sad clown above your new friend's sofa, for instance. You remember which aisle has the toothpaste and which aisle has the energy bars at your new pharmacy. You feel just as awestruck by the Grand Canyon on your second vacation there, but for different reasons.

In the same way, if you take a second look at the novel you have just read, after going through the process of active reading outlined above, you may see it in a slightly different light. You may understand the events better after journaling about them. You may be less distracted by the old-fashioned language of the narration after having looked up the unfamiliar words. You may be less blinded to the villainy of one of the characters after you have discussed her dishonesty with a reading partner.

Taking a second look doesn't mean rereading word for word. It just means skimming through, looking again at your marginal notes, going over key passages in the text, or reading a line of dialogue you have read before and seeing something new in it. It takes far less time than re-watching your favorite DVD, and the effort is well worth the new insights you'll gain.

Your relationship with an author doesn't have to end with just one novel. Check the library or bookstore for other novels by the same author. Not only will your familiarity with the author's body of work help you in class discussions and writing assignments, it will allow you to enter a successive number of diverse worlds, each seen through the unique eyes of one writer. When you find novelists whose viewpoint you can appreciate, you're definitely going to want to hear from them again.

Putting this chapter to work

Apply this chapter to the novel you are reading by asking yourself the following questions:

- When I preview this novel, what parts do I find?
- What do the parts I preview, for example, the introduction, tell me about what to expect from this novel?
- Am I creating my own system of markup for this novel? How is it working?
- Am I keeping a journal as I read this novel? Do I find it helpful? If so, how?
- Have I discussed this novel with others who are reading it? If so, are their views different from or similar to mine?
- Does this novel have a twist ending or a complex overall plot? If so, do I think that taking a second look will help me understand it on a deeper level?
- Have I tried downloading an electronic version of this novel? What are the pros and cons, in my experience so far, of reading and note-taking electronically?
- Am I writing about personal experiences connected with events in this novel? Does doing so help me get more deeply involved in my reading? Why or why not?
- Am I making any predictions about what might happen next in the novel? Are my predictions turning out to be accurate? Or am I surprised or even shocked by the novel's events?

5

Discover Ideas for Writing about Novels

In this chapter, you will:

- Identify a variety of techniques to generate ideas for writing about novels
- Build up an arsenal of favorite techniques for future use in college writing
- Learn to trust your own ideas, viewpoints, and emotions when coming up with ideas for writing about novels

This is a guide to reading a novel, not a guide to writing an essay or other college writing assignment about a novel. Your instructors will give you the tools and blueprints to build arguments about what you read. Why this chapter, then? Because reading actively can't help but light a spark in readers' minds, kindling new ideas.

Before that fire starts to die down—life intervenes—you'll thank yourself later if you explore some of the ideas your reading has generated. Not only can you draw on some of your creative thinking later on in college, when you are called upon to write about the novel you've just read. You can also get in the habit of conjuring up ideas to write about in a pinch—when faced with a timed essay test, for example.

Following are some suggestions for discovering ideas for writing about novels. These suggestions are just that—suggestions. Plus, they can be fun to do just for the sake of doing them. But they also invite you to head in the direction of formal college writing about novels in the future.

Thesaurus search

Choose a word from the novel's title or from a key passage or premise. If you have just read *Frankenstein*, what about the word *monster*? Go to a thesaurus (the print reference books in the library are best, but a thesaurus in Word or online could work) and look up the word. You'll probably see more variety in its synonyms (words with similar meanings) than you expected.

Although *monster* sounds like a bad thing, in one sense it is just an adjective meaning "huge" or "colossal," not necessarily a terrible thing to be. In another sense, it means a fiend, a brute, a freak of nature. What could these words and their overlapping and opposing meanings tell you about Dr. Frankenstein and his unfortunate creation? Which words seem to fit best, or shed new light on the novel's theme? How could you use the new definitions of *monster* in a paper about the novel?

Similes

You probably already know that a simile is a way of drawing a comparison using the words *like* or *as*: Her anger was like thunder; The rain was like a lullaby; Her true intentions were as transparent as glass.

You can use similes to generate ideas to write about by filling in these blanks with images or ideas from the novel:

_____ is like _____ .

Fill in the first blank with a character name, or some other term or concept from the novel, like its setting or its premise. Next, fill in the second blank with as many different ideas and images as you can, seeing how many you can come up with. Then go over them and circle the ones you think could be developed in writing.

For example, using a character from *Jane Eyre*:

- *Rochester* is like *an erupting volcano*.
- *Rochester* is like *a spoiled little boy*.
- *Rochester* is like *a thief robbing Jane of her affections and her dignity*.

- *Rochester* is like *a king in Jane's inexperienced eyes.*
- *Rochester* is like *a jailer, keeping his first wife captive.*
- *Rochester* is like *a prisoner in a failed marriage.*
- *Rochester* is like *an eagle, proud and untamed, just like Jane.*

Freewriting

You may be familiar with freewriting as an uncensored flow of thoughts onto the page or computer screen. But you can also freewrite on a topic. It's often called focused freewriting. Choose some aspect of your novel, for example, the setting, and freewrite about it. Highlight the sentences or phrases that contain a discovery or an insight. Choose one and write it at the top of a page, then freewrite again about that. You might come up with an idea you can use for a future essay assignment.

Pro and con lists

Draw a plus sign on the left side of your page, a minus sign on the right, and then place a vertical line between them. Without censoring yourself, list as many positives and as many negatives as you can about some feature of your novel.

Cubing

The cubing technique allows you to see your topic from multiple perspectives—six different angles, to be exact. You can use an actual cube, writing a task for yourself to complete, or a command to obey, on each face. Turn the cube as you respond to what's written on each side. But if you're not crafty, just use a six-item list. Consider your topic, then write your responses to the cubing commands. Here are two examples of cubing:

Example 1
1. Describe it.
2. Compare it.
3. Question it.
4. Connect it.
5. Apply it.
6. Change it.

Example 2
1. Evaluate it.
2. Cartoon it.
3. Investigate it.
4. Argue for it.
5. Argue against it.
6. Satirize it.

Rock or feather?

Playing this game using a character in your novel helps you think instinctively about him or her; if you answer the questions quickly enough, the results may surprise you. You can circle one of the associations you feel the most strongly about, then use it as a metaphor—a comparison using figurative language—in a future paper.

Read each pair of words. Circle the word in each pair that best describes the character you chose from your novel:

rock	feather
city	country
bat	ball
summer	winter
breakfast	dinner
plastic	cotton
Cadillac	Volkswagen
yes	no
Big Mac	sirloin steak
chocolate	vanilla
ball	bat
the present	the future
milk	Pepsi
flute	tuba
drama	comedy
river	pond
plant	animal
rock band	string quartet
motorcycle	bicycle

Continued on next page

Continued from previous page

cloudy sky   clear sky
TV   radio
easy chair   rocking chair

Probing questions

There's no such thing as a silly question. In fact, inspirational writer Clarissa Pinkola Estes says that questions cause the locked doors of the mind to swing open. And poet Rainer Maria Rilke says simply, "Live the question." In your active reading, you experimented with asking "What if" questions, that is, making predictions and speculating about possible outcomes of your novel.

In this exercise, ask yourself the following questions about your novel. Not all of the questions will work for you; if not, skip them and move on. But asking probing questions about your novel will help you move from a general idea about it to a more specific one that could be converted into an idea for an essay.

- What happened?
- Who did it?
- What does it look like?
- What are some examples of it?
- What is it made of?
- How does it work?
- Where did it come from?
- Why did it happen?
- What does it do?
- How is it like other things?
- How is it different from other things?
- What are its component parts?
- What category does it belong to?
- How can its parts be grouped?
- What does it feel like?
- How do others feel about it?
- What conflicts does it stir up?
- In what way is it good?
- In what way is it bad?

- Why does it exist?
- Who needs it?
- Where is it going?
- How do we know it exists?

Cluster and flow

As a student, you have probably already done clustering exercises to get ideas for writing. You draw a circle or square around a significant word or phrase, like "London in the nineteenth century," or "jealousy," or "Scout Finch." Then you draw lines radiating out from it, connecting it to other words that are related to that word or are the opposite of it.

Your clustering of various ideas together will result in what's often called a word web. Part of the power of clustering is that it frees you from the limitations of words and gets you working with patterns and connections you can easily visualize.

You can depart from the traditional cluster exercise by creating a flowchart. This works especially well with tracing causes and effects. You've probably seen humorous flowcharts, with their complex arrows and endless loops. But you can keep it fairly simple. Try to use flowchart language, in which certain types of arrows and certain shapes of boxes mean different things. Microsoft's Visio program has the tools if you want to do a flowchart on your computer, or just improvise.

Just what convoluted chain of events and psychological reactions had to take place to get Jay Gatsby from his humble beginnings to his party-central mansion to floating dead in his own swimming pool? Flowchart it. You might see some new connections:

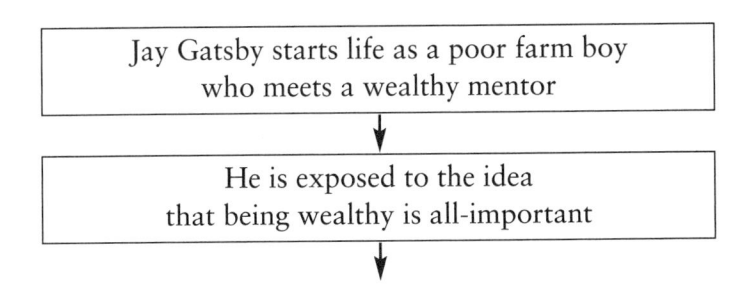

> Jay Gatsby starts life as a poor farm boy who meets a wealthy mentor
>
> ↓
>
> He is exposed to the idea that being wealthy is all-important
>
> ↓

54 • Chapter Five

```
                        ↓
┌─────────────────────────────────────────────────┐
│         He is motivated when Daisy,             │
│    a rich girl, rejects him for being poor      │
└─────────────────────────────────────────────────┘
                        ↓
┌─────────────────────────────────────────────────┐
│             Gatsby starts amassing              │
│  a fortune by becoming a criminal and gets rich │
└─────────────────────────────────────────────────┘
                        ↓
┌─────────────────────────────────────────────────┐
│                He can afford                    │
│         a mansion near Daisy's mansion          │
└─────────────────────────────────────────────────┘
                        ↓
┌─────────────────────────────────────────────────┐
│         His chances of winning her over         │
│       improve, and he expects to succeed        │
└─────────────────────────────────────────────────┘
                        ↓
┌─────────────────────────────────────────────────┐
│       He has lavish open-house parties          │
│     to make a meeting with Daisy possible       │
└─────────────────────────────────────────────────┘
                        ↓
┌─────────────────────────────────────────────────┐
│                Gatsby invites                   │
│       Daisy's cousin Nick to his parties        │
└─────────────────────────────────────────────────┘
                        ↓
┌─────────────────────────────────────────────────┐
│         He and Nick become friends              │
│     and Nick agrees to arrange a meeting        │
└─────────────────────────────────────────────────┘
                        ↓
┌─────────────────────────────────────────────────┐
│         Gatsby and Daisy meet again,            │
│          and Daisy is attracted to him          │
└─────────────────────────────────────────────────┘
                        ↓
┌─────────────────────────────────────────────────┐
│        They start having an affair,             │
│  but they aren't cautious about keeping it secret│
└─────────────────────────────────────────────────┘
                        ↓
┌─────────────────────────────────────────────────┐
│           Tom finds out his wife                │
│       and Gatsby are lovers and is furious      │
└─────────────────────────────────────────────────┘
                        ↓
```

Copyright © 2013 Pearson Education, Inc.

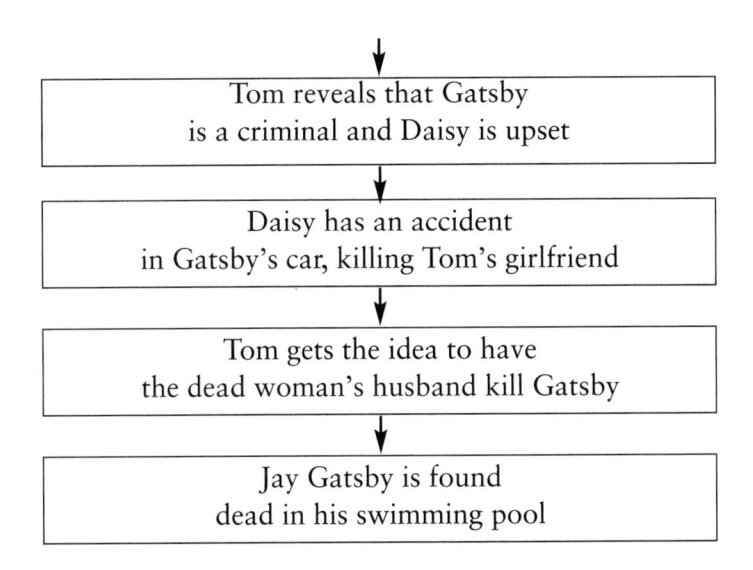

```
                    ↓
┌─────────────────────────────────────────┐
│        Tom reveals that Gatsby          │
│     is a criminal and Daisy is upset    │
└─────────────────────────────────────────┘
                    ↓
┌─────────────────────────────────────────┐
│         Daisy has an accident           │
│  in Gatsby's car, killing Tom's girlfriend │
└─────────────────────────────────────────┘
                    ↓
┌─────────────────────────────────────────┐
│        Tom gets the idea to have        │
│    the dead woman's husband kill Gatsby │
└─────────────────────────────────────────┘
                    ↓
┌─────────────────────────────────────────┐
│          Jay Gatsby is found            │
│         dead in his swimming pool       │
└─────────────────────────────────────────┘
```

In the example you just read, the cause-and-effect pattern (because of this, that happened) is not in the same order that the reader learns about it in the novel. In *The Great Gatsby*, Fitzgerald scrambles the order of events, allowing us to see them unfold in the way that Nick, an observer, would learn about them. By putting the chain of events in cause-and-effect order in the form of a flowchart, you make it easier to see the reasons behind what the characters seemingly do at random.

Note, also, that flowcharts usually show alternative choices, or options, branching off in one direction or another. You can use a flowchart to make clear to yourself the choices made by the characters, and also to play with ideas about where the plot might have gone if a character had made a different choice. For example, in *To Kill a Mockingbird*, what if Scout Finch had decided to stay home sick, rather than perform dressed as a ham in her school play on a certain fateful night?

A final suggestion for finding ideas for writing is a simple one: Trust yourself. Students have a tendency to feel unworthy when it comes to writing about great novels. After all, so many people have already written about them so well. When students doubt the validity of their own responses to literature, they tend to fall back on plot summary or repeating what critics have said, hiding what they really think. But college instructors want to hear what you think, and why you think it.

When you are discovering ideas for writing, the best place to look is inside yourself. Ultimately, the novelist writes for you, the reader. It's a communication across time and space—a message in a bottle. Answer it!

Putting this chapter to work

Apply this chapter to the novel you are reading by asking yourself these questions:

- What are my favorite idea-discovering techniques among those presented in this chapter? What, in particular, do I like about those techniques?
- What do I think are the most effective one or two techniques for getting ideas for writing to apply to the novel I'm reading?
- So far, have my idea-discovering activities uncovered anything fresh or unexpected about this novel that I can write about in a future assignment?
- How, specifically, will I use the ideas for writing I've come up with? If I plan to use them in a future paper about this novel, how exactly will I use them?
- Can I come up with any other ways of my own to generate writing ideas for this novel? Have I tried them out yet? If so, how did it go?
- Do the ideas-for-writing techniques I'm using help me understand the novel better or enjoy it more? If so, why do I think that is? If not, why not?

Copyright © 2013 Pearson Education, Inc.

ADDITIONAL TITLES IN THE **WESSKA** (WHAT EVERY STUDENT SHOULD KNOW ABOUT...) SERIES:

- *What Every Student Should Know About Avoiding Plagiarism* (ISBN 0-321-44689-5)
- *What Every Student Should Know About Citing Sources with APA Documentation* (ISBN 0-205-49923-6)
- *What Every Student Should Know About Citing Sources with MLA Documentation* (ISBN 0-205-11511-7)
- *What Every Student Should Know About Creating Portfolios* (ISBN 0-205-57250-2)
- *What Every Student Should Know About Listening* (ISBN 0-205-77807-0)
- *What Every Student Should Know About Practicing Peer Review* (ISBN 0-321-44848-0)
- *What Every Student Should Know About Preparing Effective Oral Presentations* (ISBN 0-205-50545-7)
- *What Every Student Should Know About Procrastination* (0-205-58211-7)
- *What Every Student Should Know About Reading and Studying the Social Sciences* (ISBN 0-137-14137-8)
- *What Every Student Should Know About Study Skills* (ISBN 0-321-44736-0)
- *What Every Student Should Know About Using a Handbook* (ISBN 0-205-56384-8)
- *What Every Student Should Know About Writing Across the Curriculum* (ISBN 0-205-58913-8)
- *What Every Student Should Know About World Literature* (ISBN 0-205-21166-6)
- *What Every Student Should Know About Writing About Literature* (ISBN 0-205-23655-3)
- *What Every Student Should Know About Researching Online* (ISBN 0-205-85646-2)
- *What Every Multilingual Student Should Know About Writing for College* (ISBN 0-205-23008-3)
- *What Every Student Should Know About Learning Online* (ISBN 0-205-24484-X)
- *What Every Student Should Know About Critical Reading* (ISBN 0-205-86992-0)
- *What Every Student Should Know About the Top Ten Sentence Errors* (ISBN 0-205-86546-1)